HOW TO CHANGE YOUR MIND

Learn The Tricks All Successful
People Use To Become
Incredibly Inspired

CASSANDRA CARSON

Table of Contents

Chapter 1:

How to Stop Chasing New Goals All the Time

The philosopher Alan Watts always said that life is like a song, and the sole purpose of the song is to dance. He said that when we listen to a song, we don't dance to get to the end of the music. We dance to enjoy it. This isn't always how we live our lives. Instead, we rush through our moments, thinking there's always something better, there's always some goal we need to achieve.

"Existence is meant to be fun. It doesn't go anywhere; it just is." Our lives are not about things and status. Even though we've made ourselves miserable with wanting, we already have everything we need. Life is meant to be lived. If you can't quit your job tomorrow, enjoy where you are. Focus on the best parts of every day. Believe that everything you do has a purpose and a place in the world.

Happiness comes from gratitude. You're alive, you have people to miss when you go to work, and you get to see them smile every day. We all have to do things we don't want to do; we have to survive. When you find yourself working for things that don't matter, like a big house or a fancy car, when you could be living, you've missed the point. You're playing the song, but you're not dancing.

"A song isn't just the ending. It's not just the goal of finishing the song. The song is an experience."

We all think that everything should be amazing when we're at the top, but it's not. Your children have grown older, and you don't remember the little things.

"...tomorrow and plans for tomorrow can have no significance at all unless you are in full contact with the reality of the present since it is in the present and only in the present that you live."

You feel cheated of your time, cheated by time. Now you have to make up for it. You have to live, make the most of what you have left. So you set another goal.

This time you'll build memories and see places, do things you never got the chance to do. The list grows, and you wonder how you'll get it all done and still make your large mortgage payment. You work more hours so you can do all this stuff "someday." You've overwhelmed yourself again.

You're missing the point.

Stop wanting more, be grateful for today. Live in the moment. Cherish your life and the time you have in this world. If it happens, it happens. If it doesn't, then it wasn't meant to; let it go.

"We think if we don't interfere, it won't happen."

There's always an expectation, always something that has to get done. You pushed aside living so that you could live up to an expectation that doesn't exist to anyone but you. The expectation is always there because you gave it power. To live, you've got to let it go.

You save all your money so that you can retire. You live to retire. Then you get old, and you're too tired to live up to the expectation you had of retirement; you never realize your dreams.

At forty, you felt cheated; at eighty, you are cheated. You cheated yourself the whole way through to the end.

"Your purpose was to dance until the end, but you were so focused on the end that you forgot to dance."

Chapter 2:

Be Motivated by Challenge

You have an easy life and a continuous stream of income, you are lucky! You have everything you and your children need, you are lucky! You have your whole future planned ahead of you and nothing seems to go in the other direction yet, you are lucky!

But how far do you think this can go? What surety can you give yourself that all will go well from the start to the very end?

Life will always have a hurdle, a hardship, a challenge, right there when you feel most satisfied. What will you do then?

Will you give up and look for an escape? Will you seek guidance? Or will you just give up and go down a dark place because you never thought something like this could happen to you?

Life is full of endless possibilities and an endless parade of challenges that make life no walk in the park.

You are different from any other human being in at least one attribute. But your life isn't much different than most people's. You may be less fortunate or you may be the luckiest, but you must not back down when life strikes you.

This world is a cruel place and a harsh terrain. But that doesn't mean you should give up whenever you get hit in the back. That doesn't mean you don't catch what the world throws at you.

Do you know what you should do? Look around and observe for examples. Examples of people who have had the same experiences as you had and what good or bad things did they do? You will find people on both extremes.

You will find people who didn't have the courage or guts to stand up to the challenge and people who didn't have the time to give up but to keep pushing harder and harder, just to get better at what they failed the last time.

The challenges of life can never cross your limits because the limits of a human being are practically infinite. But what feels like a heavy load, is just a shadow of your inner fear dictating you to give up.

But you can't give up, right? Because you already have what you need to overcome this challenge too. You just haven't looked into your backpack of skills yet!

If you are struggling at college, go out there and prove everyone in their wrong. Try to get better grades by putting in more hours little by little.

If people take you as a non-social person, try to talk to at least one new person each day.

If you aren't getting good at a sport, get tutorials and try to replicate the professionals step by step and put in all your effort and time if you truly care for the challenge at hand.

The motivation you need is in the challenge itself. You just need to realize the true gains you want from each stone in your path and you will find treasures under every stone.

Chapter 3:

How To Achieve Peak Performance In Your Career

What exactly do we mean by peak performance? Well, it is defined as the state when you are at your best, delivering the results and feeling in the flow. You're able to overcome the challenges and feel at ease about your work and life. Getting in a state of peak performance at work is all about being motivated, managing your energy, staying productive, and developing the proper habits. We have a finite supply of energy that we expend throughout the day, but we aren't taught how to cultivate this energy. The ultimate key to higher performance is learning how to manage your energy all through the day consciously. The challenge is, once you have reached your peak performance, you have to stay and perform in that state as constantly as possible; you have to sustain the level of peak performance. Here are some ways for you to achieve peak performance in your career.

1. Being Motivated About The Work

The best way to stay motivated I to choose something that you're both good at and love to do. Work on something that keeps you energized and motivated. When you do this type of work, you're more likely to operate in a flow state and achieve peak performance. But, as much as we like, there won't always be things that favor our interest. In those situations, it's helpful to reframe the problem that fits the "why" purpose. For example, if you are unwilling to do something, but there's an urgency, and you're bound to do it, you will find a way and energy to get with it anyway. It would be best to start focusing on the gains and benefits you will get from doing the things you dislike. This will keep you somewhat motivated to do it. Or you can ask for help from someone who loves doing the work that you hate. It's all about reframing the situations to your best interest.

2. Developing The Right Habits

Achieving peak performance is more about the actions you take and the thoughts you think. Having negative thoughts like "will I be able to do it?" or "what if he/she is better at it than me?" and so forth will only make you anxious. It will be like driving with the handbrake on, and your performance will only be a drag. Instead, try and develop positive thoughts. Get on with the attitude of "I can do it" or "I can learn from my colleagues if I mess up." Adopting such positive thoughts will give you a huge boost towards your peak performance. Behavior habits can also hurt your performance just as severely. For example, if you have a habit of arriving late, start getting ready 10-20 minutes earlier than you usually do. If you are afraid to speak up, try saying anything for the first 60 seconds, so your voice is at least heard.

3. Staying Productive

Alongside having the motivation and the right habits, try to get more work done with the same or fewer resources; whether it's time, money, energy, you'll be steps ahead. Being productive also means that you can create extra time for the next task, thinking, or simply to recharge. Banishing obstacles like procrastination and perfectionism can help you achieve your peak performance. Address the things that are holding you back. Assess and evaluate them, stay on track by planning your day the night before.

4. Managing Your Energy

You can generate more and more of your energy, that's the best thing about it. It is a renewable resource, while time is not. Therefore, it is essential to manage your energy and protect your time. One way you can manage your energy is by matching your tasks with the day that best suits you. If you are more productive and creative in the morning, start doing the more significant and more critical tasks in that time, and leave the small ones for later. The prominent energy creators revolve around your health and wellness, both physical and mental. Get a good night's sleep every day, have a proper diet, and exercise regularly.

5. Be Consistent

The single most important thing you can do for your career is to show up every day. No skill or talent can beat the power of consistency. Being consistent will continue to maximize your potential for peak performance and give you an upper hand over those who tend to take the opposite of consistency. As you continue to learn and apply the new lessons you have learned from your experience at work, your ability to perform at peak will stay on the upward side of the scale longer than expected.

Conclusion

Above everything else, we should remember that sustaining peak performance at work doesn't have to be your hit or miss gamble. You should know your numbers and plot out strategies for compounding improvements and set measurable goals to work. This will give you not only a progressive routine but also some direction and clarity. Embrace the momentum tum to stay in the flow state longer than your co-workers or the last time you did. Track your performance and continue to beat your current record to keep yourself motivated and full of confidence.

Chapter 4:

When It Is Time To Let Go and Move On (Career)

Today we're going to talk about a topic that I hope will motivate you to quit that job that you hate or one that you feel that you have nothing more to give anymore.

For the purpose of this video, we will focus mainly on career as I believe many of you may feel as though you are stuck in your job but fear quitting because you are afraid you might not find a better one.

For today's topic, I want to draw attention to a close friend of mine who have had this dilemma for years and still hasn't decided to quit because he is afraid that he might not get hired by someone else.

In the beginning of my friend's career, he was full of excitement in his new job and wanted to do things perfectly. Things went pretty smoothly over the course of the first 2 years, learning new things, meeting new friends, and getting settled into his job that he thought he might stay on for a long time to come seeing that it was the degree that he had pursued in university. However when the 3rd year came along, he started to feel jaded with his job. Everyday he would meet ungrateful and sometimes mean customers who were incredibly self-entitled. They would be rude and he started dreading going to work more and more each day. This aspect of the job wore him down and he started to realise that he wasn't happy at all with his work.

Having had a passion for fitness for a while now, he realized that he felt very alive when he attended fitness classes and enjoyed working out and teaching others how to work out. He would fiddle with the idea of attending a teacher training course that would allow him to be a professional and certified fitness coach.

As his full time job started to become more of a burden, he became more serious about the prospect of switching careers and pursuing a new one entirely. At his job, realized that the company wasn't generous at all with the incentives and gruelling work hours, but he stayed on as he was afraid he wouldn't find another job in this bad economy. The fear was indeed real so he kept delaying trying to quit his job. Before he knew it 3 years more had passed and by this time he full on dreaded every single minute at his job.

It was not until he made that faithful decision one day to send in his resignation letter and to simultaneously pay for the teacher training course to become a fitness instructor did his fortunes start to change for him. The fortunes in this wasn't about money. It was about freedom. It was about growth. And it was about living.

We all know deep in our hearts when it is time to call it quits to something. When we know that there is nothing more that we can possibly give to our job. That no amount of time more could ever fulfill that void in us. That we just simply need to get out and do something different.

You see, life is about change. As we grow, our priorities change, our personalities change, our expectations change, and our passions and our interests change as well. If we stay in one place too long, especially in a field or in something that we have hit a wall at, we will feel stuck, and we will feel dread. We will feel that our time spent is not productive and we end up feeling hopeless and sorry for ourselves.

Instead when we choose to let go, when we choose to call time on something, we open up the doors for time on other ventures, and other adventures. And our world becomes brighter again.

I challenge each and everyone of you to take a leap of faith. You know deep in your hearts when it is time to move on from your current job and find the next thing. If you dont feel like you are growing, or if you feel that you absolutely hate your job because there is no ounce of joy that you can derive from it, move on immediately. Life is too short to be spending 10 hours of your life a day on something that you hate, that sucks the living soul out of you. Give yourself the time and space to explore, to find some other path for you to take. You will be surprised what might happen when you follow your heart.

I hope you learned something today, take care and I'll see you in the next one.

Chapter 5:

Five Habits For A Beautiful Life

A beautiful life means different things to different people. However, there are some things that we can all agree about. It is a happy one. Some of us have chased this kind of life but it has proven elusive to the brink of throwing in the towel. We play a greater role in designing a beautiful life for ourselves than others do in our lives.

Here are five habits for a beautiful life:

1. Live The Moment

This is not a call to carelessness. The focal point is to cherish the present moment. We are often distracted by our past experiences even in times when we ought to celebrate our current wins. The present is beautiful because we can influence it.

A beautiful life is joyous and the envy of those who cannot experience it. Savor the present completely and do not be entangled in the past. The past will withhold you from leveraging the opportunities popping up presently. Every saint has a past and every sinner has a future. You can shape the future by living in the moment and not dwelling in the past.

Worrying about the future is not beneficial. If you can change a situation, why worry? If you cannot also change anything, why worry? It is pointless to take the burden of occurrences that are yet to happen. Enjoy your present successes while you can and lead the beautiful life you have been dreaming of.

2. Plan Wisely

Like everything invaluable, a beautiful life should be planned for. Planning is an integral part of determining whether a beautiful flawless life is achievable or not. It is not an event but a process that requires meticulous attention.

Planning entails extensive allocation of resources to life priorities. You should get your priorities right for things to run smoothly. In planning, your judgment and conscience should be as clear as a cloudless night. Any conflict of interest that could arise will jeopardize the attainment of a beautiful life - the ultimate goal.

We may be forced to make some painful sacrifices along the way and possibly give up short-time pleasures for long-term comfort. It may bring some discomfort but is worth the attainment of a beautiful life. Planning is a heavy price that must be made a routine to anyone aspiring to this magnificent dream.

3. Pursue Your Purpose

Your purpose is the sole reason that keeps you going in life. You should pursue what motivates you to keep chasing your dreams. A beautiful life is one of fulfillment. Your purpose will bring it effortlessly if you remain loyal to it.

Focusing on your purpose can be a daunting task to an undisciplined mind. Many distractions may come up to make you stray or shift goalposts. You need to be disciplined to continue treading in the narrow path of your purpose. Do not lose sight of the antelope (a beautiful life) because of a dashing squirrel (distractions).

Living a life of purpose will satisfy you because you will willfully do what brings you joy; not what circumstances have forced you to. A cheerful way to live each day like it is your last is by finding pleasure in your routine activities and by extension, your purpose. Pursue it boldly!

4. Cut Your Coat According To Your Cloth

Live within your means and cut on unnecessary costs. Many people struggle to live within a particular social class that they are not able to afford at the moment. In the process of fitting in, they incur unmanageable debt.

A beautiful life does not mean one of luxury. It is stress-free and affordable within your space. It is unimaginable that one will wear himself/herself out to live a lifestyle beyond reach. Societal pressure should not push you to the brink of self-destruction as you try to fit in other people's shoes.

Even as you work towards your goals, do not suffocate yourself to please other people. Accept your financial status and make your budget within it. You will have an authentic and beautiful life.

5. Share Your Life With Your Loved Ones

We all have our families and loved ones. Our parents, siblings, spouses, and children should share our lives with us. It is beautiful and desirable that we intertwin our social and personal lives. The warmth and love of our families will put a smile on our faces despite any challenges.

Often, our families are the backbone of our emotional support. We retreat to them when we are wounded by the struggles of life and they nurse us back to health. Their presence and contribution to our lives are immeasurable. Family does not necessarily mean you have to be related by blood.

Some people are strong pillars in our lives and have seen us through hard times. Over time, they have become part of our family. We should share our lives with them and treasure each moment. We would be building a beautiful life for ourselves and the upcoming generations.

These are five habits we need to develop for a beautiful life. We only live once and should enjoy our lifetime by all means.

Chapter 6:

Why You Are Amazing

When was the last time you told yourself that you were amazing? Was it last week, last month, last year, or maybe not even once in your life?

As humans, we always seek to gain validation from our peers. We wait to see if something that we did recently warranted praise or commendation. Either from our colleagues, our bosses, our friends, or even our families. And when we don't receive those words that we expect them to, we think that we are unworthy, or that our work just wasn't good enough. That we are lousy and under serving of praise.

With social media and the power of the internet, these feelings have been amplified. For those of us that look at the likes on our Instagram posts or stories, or the number of followers on Tiktok, Facebook, or Snapchat, we allow ourselves to be subjected to the validation of external forces in order to qualify our self-worth. Whether these are strangers who don't know you at all, or whoever they might be, their approval seems to matter the most to us rather than the approval we can choose to give ourselves.

We believe that we always have to up our game in order to seek happiness. Everytime we don't get the likes, we let it affect our mood for the rest of the day or even the week.

Have you ever thought of how wonderful it is if you are your best cheerleader in life? If the only validation you needed to seek was from yourself? That you were proud of the work you put out there, even if the world disagrees, because you know that you have put your heart and soul into the project and that there was nothing else you could have done better in that moment when you were producing that thing?

I am here to tell you that you are amazing because only you have the power to choose to love yourself unconditionally. You have the power to tell yourself that you are amazing. and that you have the power to look into yourself and be proud of how far you came in life. To be amazed by the things that you have done up until this point, things that other people might not have seen, acknowledged, or given credit to you for. But you can give that credit to yourself. To pat yourself on the back and say "I did a great job".

I believe that we all have this ability to look inwards. That we don't need external forces to tell us we are amazing because deep down, we already know we are.

If nobody else in the world loves you, know that I do. I love your courage, your bravery, your resilience, your heart, your soul, your commitment, and your dedication to live out your best life on this earth. Tell yourself each and everyday that you deserve to be loved, and that you are loved.

Go through life fiercely knowing that you don't need to seek happiness, validations, and approval from others. That you have it inside you all along and that is all you need to keep going.

Chapter 7:

Six Habits of The Mega-Rich

There are rich people then there are the mega-rich. The distinction between them is as clear as day. The former are still accumulating their wealth while the latter is beyond that. Their focus is no longer on themselves but humanity. Their view of things is through the prism of business and not employment. Their business enterprises are well established and their level of competition is unmatched. They are at the top of the pyramid and have a clear view of things below.

Here are six habits of the mega-rich:

1. They Have a Diversified Investment Portfolio

The mega-rich are ardent followers of the saying "do not put all your eggs in one basket." They have stakes in every type of business across many world economies beginning with their country. Their patriotism makes them not leave out their countries when they do business. With diversified risk across various sectors of the economy, they can remain afloat even during tough economic times. Their companies and businesses also yield high returns because of proper management and their diversification.

2. They Are Generous

The mega-rich people are generous to a fault. They run foundations and non-governmental organizations in their name with a cause to help humanity. It indicates their generosity and desire to help the most vulnerable and needy in society. Generosity is a hard trait to trace these days and it distinguishes the mega-rich from kind people.

The generosity of mega-rich people seeks to help the needy permanently by showing them how to fish instead of giving them fish. Such an act liberates families from poverty and promises a brighter future to the younger generation.

3. They Are Neither Petty Nor Trivial

Pettiness is not the character of mega-rich people. They do not have time for small squabbles and fights. Instead, they use their energy in pursuit of more productive goals. Their minds always think of their next big move and ways to improve their businesses. They do not have time to engage in non-issues.

Mega-rich investors do not undertake trivial investments. Their businesses are major leaving people marveling at its grandiose. Jeff Benzos took a trip to space and the world was amazed. The impact the ilk of Benzos has in the world economy is unmatched; securities exchanges and global trade shakes whenever such people make a business move.

4. They Have A Clean Public Image

The mega-rich people manage to maintain a scandalous-free public image. This is crucial for their success. When was the last time you came across a character-damaging story of a wealthy person? It is difficult to recall. Perception tends to stick in the minds of people more than reality. This makes it important for them to guard their reputation with their life.

If you are on the path of joining the exclusive club of the mega-rich, begin cleaning up your reputation if it is a mess. Build a new public image that will portray you as a better person to the world. Mega-rich people intimidate by their angel-like reputations and immense influence on their social status.

5. They Have Great Character

A man's character precedes his reputation. Every wealthy person upgrades his/hers. The mega-rich treasure character too much because they are unable to buy it at any price. It is invaluable. Characterlessness is a type of poverty only curable the hard way. There is no shortcut to it except tireless and intentional channeling of your efforts to strengthen it.

A great character is an asset envied by the great and mighty because most of them fall short of it. There are untold stories of the efforts mega-rich people put to build their character. This has formed part of their routine and life habit.

6. They Champion Global Causes

Mega-rich people are champions of social justice and world causes like climate change and global warming. They give their contribution towards global causes without any self-interest. They are at the forefront offering support in whatever capacity.

They invest in these worthy causes because of the duty of corporate social responsibility they owe the world. It is not a debt they pay but an act they do gladly because they have the best interest of the world at heart.

These six habits of the mega-rich have formed their lifestyle. Walk in their footsteps if you want to become like them. You will command respect from everybody. Your business moves shall determine world market trends and you shall set the pace in every sector of the economy.

Chapter 8:

Why You're Demotivated By A Values Conflict

Every human being, in fact, every organism in this universe is different from even the same member of their species. Every one of us has different traits, likes, dislikes, colors, smells, interests so it's natural to have a difference of opinion.

It's natural to have a different point of view. It's natural and normal to have a different way of understanding. And it's definitely normal for someone else to disagree with your ways of dealing with things.

Most of us don't want to see someone disagreeing with us because we have this tricky little fellow inside of us that we call EGO.

Our ego makes us feel disappointed when we see or hear someone doing or saying something better than us. We cannot let go of the fact that someone might be right or that someone might be Okay with being wrong and we can't do a single thing about it.

This conflict of values occurs within ourselves as well. We want to do one thing but we cannot leave the other thing as well. We want to have something but we cannot keep it just because we don't have the resources to maintain them.

This feeling of 'want to have but cannot have' makes us susceptible to feelings of incompleteness ultimately making us depressed. The reality of life is that you can't always get what you want. But that doesn't make it a good enough reason to give up on your dreams or stop thinking about other things too.

Life has a lot to offer to us. So what if you can't have this one thing you wanted the most. Maybe it wasn't meant for you in the first place. Nature has a way of giving you blessings even when you feel like you have nothing.

Let's say you want something but your mind tells you that you can't have it. So what you should do is to find alternative ways to go around your original process of achieving that thing and wait for new results. What you should do is to give up on the idea altogether just because you have a conflict within your personality.

You cannot let this conflict that is building within you get a hold of you. Clear your mind, remove all doubts, get rid of all your fears of failure or rejection, and start working from a new angle with a new perspective. Set new goals and new gains from the same thing you wanted the first time. This time you might get it just because you already thought you had nothing to lose.

This feeling of 'No Regret' will eventually help you get over any situation you ever come across after a fight with your inner self. This feeling can help you flourish in any environment no matter what other people say or do behind your back.

Nothing can bring you peace but yourself. Nothing holds you back but your other half within you.

Chapter 9:

Consistency

Today we're going to talk about a very important topic that I believe is one of the core principles that we should all strive to integrate into our lives. And that is consistency.

What does consistency mean to you when you hear that word? For me previously when I kept hearing people say that I would need to stay consistent in this and that, it did not ring any bells in me and i brushed it off thinking it was just another productivity word similar to work hard, be positive and so on. However it was only when I start doing more digging that I realized that many successful people in life actually attributed consistency as being the key factor that led to their success. That it was that one quality they possessed in their work ethic that allowed them to surpass their competition. That they had set out a plan and stuck to it consistency over days, months, years, and even decades until they finally achieved their goals.

You see for many of us, consistency is something that i believe we all struggle with. Whether it be going to the gym, putting in the effort to work out, going for trainings, health wise or work related, studying, practicing an instrument, especially things we find to be not so enjoyable to do, we just do not show up consistently enough to produce results that are satisfactory let alone ones that we are proud of. And we complain that our body doesn't look good, that we are getting nowhere with learning a new instrument, or maybe that we have plateaued in the area that we most wish to desire to move forward in, work or play.

You see, your level of consistency is directly correlated with the amount of time you actually spend on an activity. And if your consistency drops, it is no wonder that your performance drops as well as you are not putting in the adequate amount of time to actually progress forward. As the saying goes, practice makes perfect. And Practice takes time. And time requires consistency.

Highly successful figures in any field, be it sports or the business world, from roger Federer, Lionel Messi, Michael jordan, Kobe Bryant, to Elon Musk, Bill Gates, Steve Jobs, they possess a strong vision for themselves and their consistency is a tool for their success. They would not hesitate to put every ounce of their time and energy into being the best in their field by showing up every single day for practice or for work, to get better each day and to crush their opinion. What they lack in skill, they make up for in consistency in practice. And they improve much faster than their opponents as a result, keeping them at the very top level of their game.

With the knowledge that consistency was the key to success for many entrepreneurs and businessmen, i decided to try it out for myself. Previously I was erratic in my work schedule. I always wandered around my tasks and never put in the effort to put in a set number of hours every day. I felt that my body wasn't getting any fitter, my tennis was average at best, and my income never really went anywhere. In all areas of my life, it felt like i had reached a ceiling.

After making the change to becoming more consistent in everything that I did, I saw a marked improvement in all areas that I had struggled with previously. My body started taking shape, my tennis game improved, and my income grew as well. The thing is, i hadn't done anything different apart from making it a daily habit and routine of putting in more hours into each task, showing up for more gym sessions, showing up for more tennis games, showing up for more hours at work, and consistently putting out more content. While gradual, these hours slowly added up and I saw a breakthrough. And I was surprised at how one small little change in how I approached life actually benefited me. I felt happier that i was improving in all these areas, and it had a snowball effect of actually compounding over time. Sooner or later i was beating my peers in all areas that I was once level with.

I challenge each and everyone of you to make consistency one of your core philosophies in life. To approach each and every task, project, or mission you embark on with a level of consistency unmatched by those around you. I am sure you will be very surprised at what you can achieve with just this one simple tweak in everything that you do.

Chapter 10:

The Problem With Immediate

Gratification

In today's topic we are going to talk about something that I am sure most of us struggle with every single day, myself included. I hope that by the end of this video, you will be able to make better decisions for yourself to maybe think further ahead rather than trying to get gratification right away.

There will be 5 areas that I want to talk about. Finance, social media, shopping, fitness, and career.

Alright if you're ready let's begin.

Let's start with the one thing that i think most of us will find it hard to resist. Shopping. For many of us, buying things can be a form of happiness. When we want something, our dopamine levels rise, and our attention is solely focused on acquiring that object whatever it may be. The anticipation of getting something is something very exciting and our bodies crave that sense of gratification in getting that product. Shopping can also be a form of distraction, maybe from work or from feeling stressed out. Shopping can also arise from boredom and the desire within us to satisfy our cravings for wanting things begins to consume us. This creates a real problem because after we attain the item, often we are not satisfied and start looking for the next thing. This creates a never ending cycle of seeking gratification immediately at the expense of our bank account. And we are soon left with a big hole in the wallet without realising it.

Before I talk about the solutions to this problem, i want to address the other 4 areas on the list.

The next one is social media. We tend to gravitate towards social media apps when we want to fill our time out of most probably boredom. At times when we are supposed to be working, instead of blocking out time to stay focused on the task at hand, we end up clicking on Instagram or Facebook, trying to see if there are any new updates to look at provided to us by the algorithm. Social media companies know this and they exploit our feeble nature with this cheap trick. Everytime we try to refresh a page, we seek immediate gratification. And we create within us a terrible habit hundreds of times a day, checking for updates that wastes hours away from our day.

The next area that maybe isn't so common is in the area of fitness. Instead of laying out a long term plan to improve our health and fitness through regular exercise and choosing healthy foods, we tend to want things happening for us immediately. We think and crave losing 10 pounds by tomorrow and set unrealistic targets that easily lets us down. Hence we seek for quick fix solutions that aim to cut short this process. We may end up trying to take slimming pills, or looking for the next extreme fad or diet to get to our goals quicker. Many of them not ending the right way and can be potentially harmful for our health. For those that cannot control what they eat, in reverse they may seek immediate gratification by bingeing on a fast food meal, ice cream, chocolates, or whatever foods brings them the quickest source of comfort. Many a times at the expense of their weight. All these are also very harmful examples of immediate gratification.

The 4th area I want to talk about is something of bigger importance. And this may not resonate with everybody, but it is about having a career that also focuses on building a side stream of passive income rather than one that focuses on active income. You see active income is static. When we work, we get a pay check at the end of every month. We look forward to that paycheck and that becomes our gratification. But when we stop working, our income stream ceases as well. This desire to keep that paycheck every month keeps us in the jobs that we ate. And we only look towards our jobs as a means to an end, to get that gratification every month in X amounts of dollars. And for many of us who uses shopping as a way to fill the void left by our jobs, we end up using that Hard earned money to gratify ourselves even more, taking up loans and mortgages to buy more and more things. If this is you, you are definitely not alone.

The final area I want to address in the area of finance. And that goes hand in hand with spending money as well. You see for many of us, we fail to see the power that compounding and time has on our finances. When we spend money today instead of saving or investing it, we lose the potential returns that investments can do for our capital. While it may be fun for us to spend money now to acquire things, it may instead bring us 10x the joy knowing that this $1000 that we have invested could end up becoming $100000 in 30 years when it is time for us to retire. The effects of compounding are astonishing and I urge all of you to take a closer look at investing what you have now as you might be surprised at the amounts of returns you can get in 30-50 years or even sooner.

So where does this lead us in our fight against instant gratification? From the areas we have described, immediate gratification always seem to have a direct negative consequence. When we choose to satisfy our cravings for wanting things fast right now, we feed our inner desires that just keeps craving more. The point is that we will never be satisfied.

If however we take a long-term approach to things and make better decisions to delay our reward, many a times that feeling will return us more than 2 fold than if we had taken it immediately. The problem is that most of us do not possess this sort of patience. Our instinct tells us that now is the best time. But history and the law of life has repeatedly shown us that that is not always true. For many things in our life, things actually gets better with time. The more time you give yourself to heal from a heartbreak, the better it will get. The more time you invest your money, the greater the returns. The more time you spend time on doing something you love, the more happiness you will feel. The more time you put into eating moderately and exercising regularly, the faster you will see your body and health take shape. The more you resist turning on the social media app, the more you will find you won't need its attention after a while. The more time you spend with friends, the deeper the friendship.

The moral of the story in all of this is that giving yourself enough time is the key to success. Trying to get something quick and easy is not always the best solution to everything. You have to put in the time and energy required to see the fruits of your labour. And that is a law that we all have to realise and apply if we want to see true success. Rome isn't built in a day, so why would anything else be? We shouldn't rush through everything that we do expecting fast results and instant gratification.

So i challenge each and everyone of you to take a good look at the areas of your life that you expect fast results and things to happen immediately. See if any of the things that I have mentioned earlier resonates with you and see if you can modify the way you acquire things. I believe that with a little effort, we all can look towards a more rewarding path to success.

Chapter 11:

Things That Spark Joy

I'm sure you've heard the term "spark joy", and this is our topic of discussion today that I am going to borrow heavily from Marie Kondo.

Now why do I find the term spark joy so fascinating and why have i used it extensively in all areas of my life ever since coming across that term a few years ago?

When I first watched Marie Kondo's show on Netflix and also reading articles on how this simple concept that she has created has helped people declutter their homes by choosing the items that bring joy to them and discarding or giving away the ones that don't, I began my own process of decluttering my house of junk from clothes to props to ornaments, and even to furniture.

I realised that many things that looked good or are the most aesthetically pleasing, aren't always the most comfortable to use or wear. And when they are not my go to choice, they tend to sit on shelves collecting dust and taking up precious space in my house. And after going through my things one by one, this recurring theme kept propping up time and again. And i subconsciously associated comfort and ease of use with things that spark joy to me. If I could pick something up easily without hesitation to use or wear, they tend to me things that I gravitated to naturally, and these things began to spark joy when i used them. And when i started getting rid of things that I don't find particularly pleased to use, i felt my house was only filled with enjoyable things that I not only enjoyed looking at, but also using on a regular and frequent basis.

This association of comfort and ease of use became my life philosophy. It didn't apply to simply just decluttering my home, but also applied to the process of acquiring in the form of shopping. Every time i would pick something up and consider if it was worthy of a purpose, i would examine whether this thing would be something that I felt was comfortable and that i could see myself utilising, and if that answer was no, i would put them down and never consider them again because i knew deep down that it would not spark joy in me as I have associated joy with comfort.

This simple philosophy has helped saved me thousands of dollars in frivolous spending that was a trademark of my old self. I would buy things on the fly without much consideration and most often they would end up as white elephants in my closet or cupboard.

To me, things that spark joy can apply to work, friends, and relationships as well. Expanding on the act of decluttering put forth by Marie Kondo. If the things you do, and the people you hang out with don't spark you much joy, then why bother? You would be better off spending time doing things with people that you actually find fun and not waste everybody's time in the process. I believe you would also come out of it being a much happier person rather than forcing yourself to be around people and situations that bring you grief.

Now that is not to say that you shouldn't challenge yourself and put yourself out there. But rather it is to give you a chance to assess the things you do around you and to train yourself to do things that really spark joy in you that it becomes second nature. It is like being fine tuned to your 6th sense in a way because ultimately we all know what we truly like and dislike, however we choose to ignore these feelings and that costs us time effort and money.

So today's challenge is for you to take a look at your life, your home, your friendships, career, and your relationships. Ask yourself, does this thing spark joy? If it doesn't, maybe you should consider a decluttering of sorts from all these different areas in your life and to streamline it to a more minimalist one that you can be proud of owning each and every piece.

Take care and I'll see you in the next one.

Chapter 12:

How Smart Do You Have To Be To Succeed

How smart do you have to be to succeed? How intelligent do you need to be to become a successful entrepreneur? How well does your training program need to be to become an elite athlete? How perfect does your weight loss program need to be to burn fat?

We don't often ask ourselves questions, but they are built into our beliefs and actions about many phases of life. We often think that we aren't succeeding because we haven't found the right strategy or because we weren't born with the right talents. Perhaps that is true. Or, perhaps there is an untold side of the story.

THRESHOLD THEORY

The surprising discovery that came out of Terman's study is best described by creativity researcher and physician Nancy Andreasen as Threshold Theory...

"Although many people continue to equate intelligence with genius, a crucial conclusion from Terman's study is that having a high IQ is not equivalent to being highly creative. Subsequent studies by other researchers have reinforced Terman's conclusions, leading to what's known as the threshold theory, which holds that above a certain level, intelligence doesn't have much effect on creativity: most creative people are pretty smart, but they don't have to be that smart, at least as measured by conventional intelligence

tests. An IQ of 120, indicating that someone is very smart but not exceptionally so, is generally considered sufficient for creative genius."

THRESHOLD THEORY IN EVERYDAY LIFE

If you look around, you'll see that the Threshold Theory applies to many things in life. There is a minimum threshold of competence that you need to develop in nearly any endeavor. Success is rarely as simple as "just work harder."

Beyond that threshold, however, the difference is between those who put in the work and those who get distracted. Once you have a basic grasp of the right things to do, it becomes about the consistency of doing the right things more often. Once you understand the fundamentals, it comes down to your habits.

WRITING

Assuming you understand the core principles of writing and the basics of grammar, what determines your ability to write well more than anything else is writing a lot. Once you reach the threshold of writing a decent sentence, the thing that leads to success is writing more.

ENTREPRENEURSHIP

Assuming you know what the most important metric is for your business, what makes the biggest difference is focusing on that metric every day. Once you cross the basic threshold of knowing what to work on, the most important thing is continuing to work on that one thing and not something else.

If you're brand new to an area, then it's possible you haven't learned enough to cross the threshold yet. But for most of us, we know what works, and we have enough knowledge to make progress. It's not about being more intelligent or more skilled, and it's about overcoming distraction and doing the work that already works.

Chapter 13:

How To Not Live Your Life In Regret

Today we're going to talk about a simple yet profound topic that I hope will awaken something in you today if you have been sleeping on the wheel of your life. I hope that with this video, I can help you to stop wasting precious time and to keep doing the things that you've always said you wanted to do right now this day. Not tomorrow, but today.

Before we go any further, I want you to write down the things you wish to accomplish before you die. It can be as small as saying I love you to your mom and dad, to something bigger like quitting your job to find something you are passionate about, to leisurely things such as travelling to XXX countries by whatever age. To things such as picking up an instrument that you've always wanted to learn but told yourself you just didn't have the time or that you wont be able to do it, or other things such as making new friends, starting a family, or literally anything under the sun.

I want you to write these things down no matter how big or small, and make them a bucket list of sorts. Many people think that a bucket list is always a leisure thing, but many a times, our bucket list could be more significant in that it is something that we don't just want to do, but need to do.

We may not fill every single thing on that bucket list, but if we can even do half of them, we can say that at least we have tried and we don't regret a single thing. The fact that we attempted is sometimes good enough, it is definitely better than not even trying and living with the guilt of "what if".

Now that we have got this list down. I'm going to jump right into the one thing that will help us put all of this into perspective. And help us truly see what matters at the top of our list. And I think you will be surprised that it may not have anything to do with travel and leisure, but it is the personal goals that we have been putting off.

Are you ready for it?

I want you to close your eyes right now. Find a quiet space where no one will disturb you for the next 5-10mins. I want you to pause this video if you need to at any one point. And I want you to visualise yourself at your deathbed, at the end of your life, whether you see yourself being 80, 90, 100, or even 60 or 70, if you feel that maybe u dont see yourself living a long life. Whatever it may be, I want you to picture yourself in your last moments.

Now I want you to ask yourself, what do you regret not having done in your 20s, 30s, and 40s. What is that one thing that you just couldn't live with yourself having not done, and what that greatest regret may be. Was it not committing your life to helping others, was it not pursuing your passion? Was it not being a good father, mother, child, friend, lover?

What is it? Who do you see around you? Are there any friends that are there to see you off? Are there any family members, cousins, loved ones there? Or have you not been a good person that none of them are there to see you? Are you lonely or surrounded my love? Are you happy that you've kept your word and done the things you said you would? Or do you regret not trying?

Do you feel like your heart is full because you have conquered every experience that life has to offer? Or do you regret not spending enough time outside seeing the world for what it truly is? Do you regret not moving to a country that you said you would one day, and just lived to see people live their best lives vicariously through Instagram and Facebook and YouTube? I want you to be as honest as you can with yourself about your current actions and project them forward into the future. Are they going to bring about the kind of peace that you would feel at the end of your life knowing you've done everything you possibly can and without regret?

Take some time to think about the things I said and see if you can paint a vivid picture of what they is like. Did you commit to eating healthily that you can see yourself living to a ripe old age? Or are you consuming junk food everyday that you can't even realistically see yourself being healthy past the age of 50?

As you are visualising these, I want you to write down any thoughts that passed through your head as you see these images. Are there any new priorities that you didn't know existed? Any shift in your bucket list?

Anything that jumped out to the front of the queue that you need to fix right this second? or to start doing right now?

If you are done I want you to open your eyes. How did that feel? Was it a surreal feeling to imagine yourself dying and looking back on your life, your teens, your 20s, your 30s. What were your biggest regrets and biggest accomplishments?

I want you to take this bucket list with you and take action on them. If you can prioritise them according to practicality, do it. If there are some easy tasks that you want to execute in next 6months, I want you to start them now. If your goal is to make some new friends that you can take to your golden years, I want you to start searching for them now so that you don't end up old and alone. Being lonely is one of the worst things that can happen to you, and I dont wish that on anyone. If you need to build up some friendships, dont waste time, because friendships takes time to nurture, and you don't want to end up in a situation that you don't have anyone to look for support, comfort, and simple companionship as you grow old.

I challenge each and everyone of you to live your life to the fullest, to live a life without regret, and that starts by taking action on the things that matters the most. It is not always about becoming a millionaire or a billionaire, because money can't buy everything. Money can't buy friends, it can't buy companionship, and it will not last. Build and create things that you can take with you right up to your death bed. And Remind yourself that life is short and not worth wasting.

Today we're going to talk about a topic that hopefully helps you become more aware of who you are as a person. And why do you exist right here and right now on this Earth. Because if we don't know who we are, if we don't understand ourselves, then how can we expect to other stand and relate to others? And why we even matter?

How many of you think that you can describe yourself accurately? If someone were to ask you exactly who you are, what would you say? Most of us would say we are Teachers, doctors, lawyers, etc. We would associate our lives with our profession.

But is that really what we are really all about?

Today I want to ask you not what you do, and not let your career define you, but rather what makes you feel truly alive and connected with the world? What is it about your profession that made you want to dedicated your life and time to it? Is there something about the job that makes you want to get up everyday and show up for the work, or is it merely to collect the paycheck at the end of the month?

I believe that that there is something in each and everyone of us that makes us who we are, and keeps us truly alive and full. For those that dedicate their lives to be Teachers, maybe they see themselves as an educator, a role model, a person who is in charge of helping a kid grow up, a nurturer, a parental figure. For Doctors, maybe they see themselves as healers, as someone who feels passionate about bringing life to someone. Whatever it may be, there is more to them than their careers.

For me, I see myself as a future caregiver, and to enrich the lives of my family members. That is something that I feel is one of my purpose in life. That I was born, not to provide for my family monetary per se, but to provide the care and support for them in their old age. That is one of my primary objectives. Otherwise, I see and understand myself as a person who loves to share knowledge with others, as I am doing right now. I love to help others in some way of form, either to inspire them, to lift their spirits, or to just be there for them when they need a crying shoulder. I love to help others fulfill their greatest potential, and it fills my heart with joy knowing that someone has benefitted from my advice. From what I have to say. And that what i have to say actually does hold some merit, some substance, and it is helping the lives of someone out there.. to help them make better decisions, and to help the, realise that life is truly wonderful. That is who i am.

Whenever I try to do something outside of that sphere, when what I do does not help someone in some way or another, I feel a sense of dread. I feel that what I do becomes misaligned with my calling, and I drag my feet each day to get those tasks done. That is something that I have realized about myself. And it might be happening to you too.

If u do not know exactly who you are and why you are here on this Earth, i highly encourage you to take the time to go on a self-discovery journey, however long it may take, to figure that out. Only when you know exactly

51

who you are, can you start doing the work that aligns with ur purpose and calling. I don't meant this is in a religious way, but i believe that each and every one of us are here for a reason, whether it may to serve others, to help your fellow human beings, or to share your talents with the world, we should all be doing something with our lives that is at least close to that, if not exactly that.

So I challenge each and everyone of you to take this seriously because I believe you will be much happier for it. Start aligning your work with your purpose and you will find that life is truly worth living.

Chapter 14:

7 Ways To Cultivate Emotions That Will Lead You To Greatness

Billions of men and women have walked the earth but only a handful have made their names engraved in history forever. These handful of people have achieved 'greatness' owing to their outstanding work, their passion and their character.

Now, greatness doesn't come overnight—greatness is not something you can just reach out and grab. Greatness is the result of how you have lived your entire life and what you have achieved in your lifetime. Against all your given circumstances, how impactful your life has been in this world, how much value you have given to the people around you, how much difference your presence has made in history counts towards how great you are. However, even though human greatness is subjective, people who are different and who have stood out from everyone else in a particular matter are perceived as great.

However, cultivating greatness in life asks for a 'great' deal of effort and all kinds of human effort are influenced by human emotions. So it's safe to say that greatness is, in fact, controlled by our emotions. Having said that, let's see what emotions are associated with greatness and how to cultivate them in real life:

1. Foster Gratitude

You cannot commence your journey towards greatness without being grateful first. That's right, being satisfied with what you already have in life and expressing due gratitude towards it will be your first step towards greatness. Being in a gratified emotional state at most times (if not all) will enhance your mental stability which will consequently help you perceive life in a different—or better point of view. This enhanced perception of life will remove your stresses and allow you to develop beyond the mediocrity of life and towards greatness.

2. Be As Curious As Child

Childhood is the time when a person starts to learn whatever that is around them. A child never stops questioning, a child never runs away from what they have to face. They just deal with things head on. Such kind of eagerness for life is something that most of us lose at the expense of time. As we grow up—as we know more, our interest keeps diminishing. We stop questioning anymore and accept what is. Eventually, we become entrapped into the ordinary. On the contrary, if we greet everything in life with bold eagerness, we expose ourselves to opportunities. And opportunities lead to greatness.

3. Ignite Your Passion

Passion has become a cliché term in any discussion related to achievements and life. Nevertheless, there is no way of denying the role of passion in driving your life force. Your ultimate zeal and fervor towards what you want in life is what distinguishes you to be great. Because admittedly, many people may want the same thing in life but how bad they want it—the intensity of wanting something is what drives people to stand out from the rest and win it over.

4. Become As Persistent As A Mountain

There are two types of great people on earth—1) Those who are born great and 2) Those who persistently work hard to become great. If you're reading this article, you probably belong to the later criteria. Being such, your determination is a key factor towards becoming great. Let nothing obstruct you—remain as firm as a mountain through all thick and thin. That kind of determination is what makes extraordinary out of the ordinary.

5. Develop Adaptability

As I have mentioned earlier, unless you are born great, your journey towards greatness will be an extremely demanding one. You will have to embrace great lengths beyond your comfort. In order to come out successful in such a journey, make sure that you become flexible to unexpected changes in your surroundings. Again, making yourself adaptable first in another journey in itself. You can't make yourself fit in adverse situations immediately. Adaptability or flexibility is cultivated prudently, with time, exposing yourself to adversities, little by little.

6. Confidence Is Key

Road to greatness often means that you have to tread a path that is discouraged by most. It's obvious—by definition, everybody cannot be great. People will most likely advise against you when you aspire something out of the ordinary. Some will even present logical explanations against you;especially your close ones. But nothing should waver your faith. You must remain boldly confident towards what you're pursuing. Only you can bring your greatness. Believe that.

7. Sense of Fulfilment Through Contributions

Honestly, there can be no greater feeling than what you'd feel after your presence has made a real impact on this world. If not, what else do we live for? Having contributed to the world and the people around you; this is the purpose of life. All the big and small contributions you make give meaning to your existence. It connects you to others, man and animal alike. It fulfills your purpose as a human being. We live for this sense of fulfillment and so, become a serial contributor. Create in yourself a greed for this feeling. At the end of the day, those who benefit from your contributions will revere you as great. No amount of success can be compared with this kind of greatness. So, never miss the opportunity of doing a good deed, no matter how minuscule or enormous.

In conclusion, these emotions don't come spontaneously. You have to create these emotions, cultivate them. And to cultivate these emotions, you must first understand yourself and your goals. With your eye on the prize, you have to create these emotions in you which will pave the path to your greatness. Gratitude, curiosity, passion, persistence, adaptability and fulfillment—each has its own weight and with all the emotions at play, nothing can stop you from becoming great in the truest form.

Chapter 15:

Five Habits That Make You Age Faster

We will all get old one day. A day is coming when we will not have the youthful energy we presently enjoy. Everyone desires that this day should never come or rather come very late in our lifetime. Nevertheless, it is an inevitable occurrence. We can only delay it.

Here are five habits that make you age faster:

1. Unforgiveness

Unforgiveness is like hiding fire expecting that no one will notice. Eventually, the smoke will give you away. It arises when one deeply wrongs us leaving a trail of hurt and agony that cannot easily be forgotten. The offended party will never forget what was committed against him/her. Anytime he/she sees the other person, the bad memory is re-kindled.

It is unhealthy to hold on to such bad memories. They cause mental and emotional trauma. They cause and affect your health. When your health is affected due to your unforgiveness, you bear full consequences and can only blame yourself. However subtle it may seem, unforgiveness is responsible for the fast aging of many people who harbor it.

The offender could probably have even forgotten about it and moved on with his/her life. The victim is the one who will be left bearing the brunt of the hurt. Stress will manifest on your face in the form of contortions making you appear aged than you are. Choose forgiveness always and you will lead a happier youthful life.

2. Bitterness

Bitterness is an aftermath of unforgiveness. It is a very strong emotion that succeeds unforgiveness. Regardless that it springs forth from within, bitterness manifests on the face over time. The glory on the face of a joyous person is absent on that of a bitter person.

Ever asked yourself how people can judge someone's age bracket? The youthful glamour disappears on the face of a bitter person. Some elderly people appear very youthful. The reason is that they live a bitter-free life. Such a type of lifestyle guarantees youthfulness.

Strive to be youthful and live a fulfilling life by keeping bitterness at bay. Entertaining it will increase the rate at which you age and may succumb to old-age diseases while still at a very young age.

3. Lack of Physical Exercise

Physical exercise is an important part of the human routine. It is not reserved for sports people only but everyone needs it to grow healthy. So important is exercise that it is incorporated in the education curriculum for students to observe.

Physical exercises help one become healthy and look youthful. It burns excess calories in our body and unblocks blood vessels thus increasing the efficiency of blood flow and body metabolism. Excess water, salts, and toxins are expelled from our bodies when we sweat after intense exercise.

The lack of physical exercise makes our bodies stiff and they become a fertile ground for lifestyle diseases like high blood pressure. Conversely, exercises improve our body shape and sizes by shedding extra weight. This healthy lifestyle brought by regular exercises will enable us to live a long healthy disease-free life.

4.   Poor Dieting

Dieting serves several purposes but the chief benefit of a proper dieting habit is that it gives the body important nutrients and shields it from excesses caused by human bias. Proper dieting will make you eat nutritive food that you may even not like. The benefits of nutritive meals outweigh your tastes and preferences.

Poor dieting is taking meals without considering their nutritive value or repetitively eating a meal because you love it. This habit makes you caution less with what you eat. You will ingest excess oily and fatty foods which will harm the healthy bacteria that live in your gut. It goes further to affect your heart health and immune response to diseases.

These factors directly affect the rate at which you age. Greasy foods will manifest in your skin and alter your appearance. It may also cause acne on your face. To reduce your aging rate, improve your dieting habit and supply the body with the right nutrients.

5.   Lack Of A Skincare Routine

As much as the skin is affected by the type of meals we take, a healthy skin care routine plays a major role in maintaining youthful skin. There are many celebrities globally who look younger than their age and this has a lot to do with their skincare routine.

It varies from one person to another but the fundamentals are constant - washing your face with plenty of clean water in the morning and evening. This is to remove dirt and dead cells from the skin. When one does not take care of his/her skin, aging creeps in. The face is the most visible part of the human body and it requires maximum care.

Failure to have an efficient skincare routine will entertain old age - the last item on our wish list.

Since we are now enlightened about habits that will make us age faster, the onus is on us to fight them and remain youthful.

Chapter 16:

How Not To Control Everything.

Steve Maraboli once said, "You must learn to let go. Release the stress. You were never in control anyway." Now, it goes without saying that things flow much more smoothly when you give up control when you let them be natural when you allow them to happen instead of making them happen. Being a control freak can drain so much of your mental energy without you even knowing it. It can cause you to fall into a never-ending loop of overthinking. We obsess over controlling every aspect of life without realizing the negative effects it can cause to our health, goals, and relationships. We grab them so tightly until we suffocate and kill them eventually.

Mastering the art of letting go and not controlling everything is not easy, but we should trust our instincts and know that it will be okay no matter the circumstances. We should always open ourselves to opportunities and possibilities. The path that we control and attach ourselves desperately to isn't always the right one. There would be other valuable and productive paths if we naturally and smoothly sail onto them. Letting go of control means more freedom, peace, joy, support, and connection. It will be hard at first, but once you get your hands on it, it'll become easier and easier for you.

The first and foremost thing to do is to use your imagination. We often find ourselves overthinking the worst possibilities that could happen to us. It's like using all of your energy, time and head on climbing the steepest mountain when you can take the stairs easily and free yourself from all the stress. So, the next time you find yourself in a controlling mindset, think of all the emotional and physical energy that you might drain in trying to control a simple situation. Embrace the freedom of not having to climb that mountain and just let go and wait for whatever it is that's going to happen.

Control is usually rooted in fear. But, understand that fear is merely an illusion, its false evidence may appear real, but it's very much fake. We control things because we fear what might happen if we don't. We attach ourselves to expectations and then set ourselves up for disappointment. So, focus on grounding yourself. Take a walk in the park, meditate, relax your mind. The positive energy will only flow in when the negative energy flows out.

Have a firm belief in yourself and practice saying affirmations. Deduct any self doubts that you have and keep reassuring yourself. Recognize the importance of freedom and see what it means to you. Once you start enjoying your space, the act of controlling everything will begin to annoy you.

Change your views about life. Could you work with your life, not against it? The sooner you realize that life is beautiful and on your side, the easier it will be for you not to control everything. You would be open to opportunities and would accept whatever it will give you. If life is moving you in one direction, instead of wasting your energy in resisting and fighting it, embrace it and work towards its betterment. Some things are beyond our control; only control what you can and let go of what you cannot.

Chapter 17:

Hitting Rock Bottom

Today we're going to talk about a topic that I hope none of you will have to experience at any point in your lives. It can be a devastating and painful experience and I don't wish it on my worst enemy, but if this happens to be you, I hope that in today's video I can help you get out of the depths and into the light again.

First of all, I'm not going to waste any more time but just tell you that hitting rock bottom could be your blessing in disguise. You see when we hit rock bottom, the only reason that we know we are there is because we have become aware and have admitted to ourselves that there is no way lower that we can go. That we know deep in our hearts that things just cannot get any worse than this. And that revelation can be enlightening. Enlightening in the sense that by simple law of physics, the worse that can happen moving forward is either you move sideways, or up. When you have nothing more left to lose, you can be free to try and do everything in your power to get back up again.

For a lot of us who have led pretty comfortable lives, sometimes it feels like we are living in a bubble. We end up drifting through life on the comforts of our merits that we fail to stop learning and growing as people. We become so jaded about everything that life becomes bland.

We stop trying to be better, we stop trying to care, and we that in itself could be poison. It is like a frog getting boiled gradually, we don't notice it until it is too late and we are cooked. We are in fact slowly dying and fading into irrelevance.

But when you are at rock bottom, you become painfully aware of everything. Painfully aware of maybe your failed relationships, the things you did and maybe the people you hurt that have led you to this point. You become aware that you need to change yourself first, that everything starts with growing and learning again from scratch, like a baby learning how to walk again. And that could be a very rewarding time in your life when you become virtually fearless to try and do anything in your power to get back on your feet again.

Of course all this has to come from you. That you have to make the decision that things will never stay the same again. That you will learn from your mistakes and do the right things. When you've hit rock bottom, you can slowly begin the climb one step at a time.

Start by defining the first and most important thing that you cannot live without in life. If family means the most to you, reach out to them. Find comfort and shelter in them and see if they are able to provide you with any sort of assistance while you work on your life again. I always believe that if family is the most important thing, and that people you call family will be there with you till the very end. If family is not available to you, make it a priority to start growing a family. Family doesn't mean you have to have blood relations. Family is whoever you can rely on in your darkest times. Family is people who will accept you and love you for who you are inspite of your shortcomings. Family is people that will help nurture and get you back on your own two feet again. If you don't have family, go get one.

If hitting rock bottom to you means that you feel lost in life, in your career and finance, that you maybe lost your businesses and are dealing with the aftermath, maybe your first priority is to simply find a simple part time job that can occupy your time and keep you sustained while you figure out what to do next. Sometimes all we need is a little break to clear our heads and to start afresh again. Nothing ever stays the same. Things will get better. But don't fall into the trap of ruminating on your losses as it can be very destructive on your mental health. The past has already happened and you cannot take it back. Take stock of the reasons and don't make the same mistakes again in your career and you will be absolutely fine.

If you feel like you've hit rock bottom because of a failed marriage or relationship, whether it be something you did or your partner did, I know this can be incredibly painful and it feels like you've spent all your time with someone with nothing to show for it but wasted time and energy, but know that things like that happen and that it is perfectly normal. Humans are flawed and we all make mistakes. So yes it is okay to morn over the loss of the relationship and feel like you can't sink any lower, but don't lose faith as you will find someone again.

If hitting rock bottom is the result of you being ostracised by people around you for not being a good person, where you maybe have lost all the relationships in your life because of something you did, I'm sure you know the first step to do is to accept that you need to change. Don't look to someone else to blame but look inwards instead. Find time where you can go away on your way to reflect on what went wrong. Start going through the things that people were unhappy with you about and start looking for ways to improve yourself. If you need help, I am here for you. If not, maybe you might want to seek some professional help as well to dig a little deeper and to help guide you along a better path.

Hitting rock bottom is not a fun thing, and I don't want to claim that I know every nuance and feeling of what it means to get there, but I did feel like that once when my business failed on me and I made the decision that I could only go up from here. I started to pour all my time and energy into proving to myself that I will succeed no matter what and that I will not sit idly by and feel sorry for myself. It was a quite a journey but I came out of it stronger than before and realized that I was more resourceful than I originally thought.

So I challenge each and everyone of you who feels like you've hit the bottom to not be afraid of taking action once again. To be fearless and just take that next right step forward no matter what. And I hope to see you on the top of the mountain in time to come.

Chapter 18:

How to Face Difficulties in Life

Have you noticed that difficulties in life come in gangs attacking you when you're least prepared for them? The effect is like being forced to endure an unrelenting nuclear attack.

Overcoming obstacles in life is hard. But life is full of personal challenges, and we have to summon the courage to face them. These test our emotional mettle — injury, illness, unemployment, grief, divorce, death, or even a new venture with an unknown future. Here are some strategies to help carry you through:

1. Turn Toward Reality

So often, we turn away from life rather than toward it. We are masters of avoidance! But if we want to be present—to enjoy life and be more effective in it—we must orient ourselves toward facing reality. When guided by the reality principle, we develop a deeper capacity to deal with life more effectively. What once was difficult is now easier. What once frightened us now feels familiar. Life becomes more manageable. And there's something even deeper that we gain: Because we can see that we have grown stronger, we have greater confidence that we can grow even stronger still. This is the basis of feeling capable, which is the wellspring of a satisfying life.

2. Embrace Your Life as It Is Rather Than as You Wish It to Be

The Buddha taught that the secret to life is to want what you have and do not want what you don't have. Being present means being present to the life that you have right here, right now. There is freedom in taking life as it comes to us—the good with the bad, the wonderful with the tragic, the love with the loss, and the life with the death. When we embrace it all, then we have a real chance to enjoy life, value our experiences, and mine the treasures that are there for the taking. When we surrender to the reality of who we are, we give ourselves a chance to do what we can do.

3. Take Your Time

As the story of the tortoise and the hare tells us, slow and steady wins the race. By being in a hurry, we actually thwart our own success. We get ahead of ourselves. We make more mistakes. We cut corners and pay for them later. We may learn the easy way but not necessarily the best way. As an old adage puts it: The slower you go, the sooner you get there. Slow, disciplined, incremental growth is the kind of approach that leads to lasting change.

Chapter 19:

Pressures of Social Media

Ah social media. This piece of technology has he power to either make us better people and more connected, or wreck us all completely. I want to address this topic today because I feel that social media is a tool that has uses that can impact us either negatively or positively, depending on how we use it. For the purpose of this video, we will talk about how social media can affect our self-worth and self-esteem.

For most of us, when we first hop onto social media, our goal is to connect with our friends. We hop onto Facebook and Instagram to add our friends and to see what's up in their lives, and to be involved with them digitally so to speak. We start by chatting them up and checking out their photos and posts. And we feel happy to be part of a bigger network.

However sooner or later, we get sucked into the pressure of acquiring more people to boost our profile... to get more likes... to get more followers... to become... famous. And every time we post something, we always feel inferior that we don't have as many likes as our friends. That we are somehow unpopular. Furthermore, we start comparing our lives with our friends, and we see what a wonderful life they have lived, the amazing photos that they have taken around the world, and we start wondering where we had gone wrong in our lives, and why we are in such a "terrible" state. We start to wonder if we had made a mistake in our career paths and we constantly compare ourselves to others that make ourselves feel Low.

Another pressure we face from social media is in the area of body image and self-worth. We see posts of the world of the insta-famous, their chiseled bodies, their chiseled faces, their amazing hair, amazingly toned skin and beauty standards that we just can't help but compare ourselves to. We start feeling inferior and we start to think we are not beautiful. We then look for ways to improve the way we look that always makes us feel so lousy about ourselves. What's more is that we come across posts of people with amazing houses and with money beyond our wildest imaginations and we again beat ourselves up for it. We wonder why we are not in that same place in life as them.

Every time we open the app to see these accounts, this regular and constant comparisons leaves us with terrible Low self-esteem and self-worth that manifests in us day in and day out. And over time, it becomes part of our negative outlook on our own lives.

I had subjected myself to a few of these before when I first started out on social media. It became all too easy to bow to the pressure of social media when all you are feeding your mind every single day is the same exactly self-harming thing.

It was only after I took a break from social media and had time to grow up a little bit that I started to use social media in a much healthier way.

After coming back to social media after a long hiatus, I stopped chasing likes, stop chasing new followers, and focused on merely reconnecting once again with my friends. I stopped browsing random accounts that will always get me lost in this rabbit hole and I felt much better about myself. As I grew up, I stopped comparing myself to others but rather view people who are in better places than I was as ways to inspire me. I started to fill my accounts with people that would inspire me to get me where I want to be whether it be financially or physically. This profound shift in the way I used social media actually got me fired up each day to work towards my goals.

Using social media as a tool of inspiration, I found myself excited to start making more money from each of my followers' inspirational posts. Whether it be from following tony-Robbins, accounts created by warren buffet followers, to people who were successful in YouTube and other online business platforms, I was motivated every time I logged in rather than leaving feeling worthless.

Who you follow matters and how you choose to use social media matters as well. If you choose comparison rather than inspiration, you will always feel like you are unworthy. If you view other's success as a motivator, you can choose to follow people that inspire you each and every day to get you where you want to go.

I challenge each and every one of you to align your goals with social media. Think hard about what you want to use it for. Is it a means of escape? Or is it a tool for you to get cracking on your goals. If you wish to be healthier, follow people who inspire you each day to start working out rather than those that posts photos that only serve to show off their physique. If you want to be richer, following successful people who teach you life principles to be wealthy, rather than accounts that merely show off their incredible wealth with things they buy and the branded stuff they own. If you goal is to be a better person, there are plenty of accounts that seek to inspire. Maybe Oprah Winfrey would be a good person to o follow, if she has an account.

Choose who you follow wisely because their daily posts will have a direct consequences to how you start seeing things around you.

Chapter 20:

Don't Overthink Things

Analysis Paralysis, how many of you have heard of this term before? When a decision is placed before us, many of us try to weigh the pros and cons, over and over again, day and night, and never seem to be able to come up with an answer, not even one week later.

I have been guilty of doing such a thing many times in my life, in fact many in the past month alone. What I've come to realize is that there is never going to be a right decision, but that things always work out in the end as long as it is not a rash decision.

Giving careful thought to any big decision is definitely justified. From buying a car, to a house, to moving to another state or country for work, these are big life-changing decisions that could set the course for our professional and financial future for years to come. In these instances, it is okay to take as much time as we need to settle on the right calculated choice for us. Sometimes in these situations, we may not know the right answer as well but we take a leap of faith and hope for the best and that is the only thing we can do. And that is perfectly okay.

But if we translate the time and effort we take in those big projects into daily decisions such as where to go, what to eat, or who to call, we will find ourselves in a terrible predicament multiple times a day. If we overthink the simple things, life just becomes so much more complicated. We end up over-taxing our brain to the point where it does not have much juice left to do other things that are truly important.

The goal is to keep things simple by either limiting your choices or by simply going with your gut. Instead of weighing every single pro and con before making a decision, just go. The amount of time we waste calculating could be better spent into energy for other resources.

I have found that i rarely ever make a right choice even after debating hours on end whether I should go somewhere. Because i would always wonder what if i had gone to the other place instead. The human mind is very funny thing. We always seem to think the grass could be greener on the other side, and so we are never contented with what we have in front of us right here right now.

The next time you are faced with a non-life changing decision, simply flip a coin and just go with the one that the coin has chosen for you. Don't look back and flip the coin the other way unless it is truly what your heart wants. We will never be truly happy with every single choice we make. We can only make the most of it.

Chapter 21:

Living in the Moment

Today we're going to talk about a topic that will help those of you struggling with fears and anxieties about your past and even about your future. And I hope that at the end of this video, you may be able to live a life that is truly more present and full.

So what is living in the moment all about and why should we even bother?

You see, for many of us, since we're young, we've been told to plan for our future. And we always feel like we're never enough until we achieve the next best grade in class, get into a great university, get a high paying career, and then retire comfortably. We always look at our life as an endless competition, and that we believe that there will always be more time to have fun and enjoy life later when we have worked our asses off and clawed our way to success. Measures that are either set by our parents, society, or our peers. And this constant desire to look ahead, while is a good motivator if done in moderation and not obsessively, can lead us to always being unhappy in our current present moment.

Because we are always chasing something bigger, the goal post keeps moving farther and farther away every time we reach one. And the reality is that we will never ever be happy with ourselves at any point if that becomes our motto. We try to look so far ahead all the time that we miss the beautiful sights along the way. We miss the whole point of our goals which is not to want the end goal so eagerly, but to actually enjoy the process, enjoy the journey, and enjoy each step along the way. The struggles, the sadness, the accomplishments, the joy. When we stop checking out the flowers around us, and when we stop looking around the beautiful sights, the destination becomes less amazing.

Reminding ourselves to live in the present helps us keep things in perspective that yes, even though our ultimate dream is to be this and that career wise, or whatever it may be, that we must not forget that life is precious and that each day is a blessing and that we should cherish each living day as if it were your last.

Forget the idea that you might have 30 years to work before you can tell ur self that you can finally relax and retire. Because you never know if you will even have tomorrow. If you are always reminded that life is fragile and that your life isn't always guaranteed, that you become more aware that you need to live in the moment in order to live your best life. Rid yourself of any worries, anxieties, and fears you have about the future because the time will come when it comes. Things will happen for you eventually so long as you do what you need to do each and every day without obsessing over it.

Sometimes our past failures and shortcomings in the workplace can have an adverse effect on how we view the present as well. And this cycle perpetuates itself over and over again and we lose sight of what's really important to us. Our family, our friends, our pets, and we neglect them or neglect to spend enough time with them thinking we have so much time left. But we fail to remember again that life does not always work the way we want it to. And we need to be careful not to fall into that trap that we have complete and total control over our life and how our plans would work out.

In the next video we will talk about how to live in the moment if you have anxieties and fears about things unrelated to work. Whether it be a family issue or a health issue. I want to address that in a separate topic.

Chapter 22:

Take Ownership of Yourself

What belongs to you but is used by other people more than you?
Your name.

And that's okay. People can use your name. But you must never allow yourself to lose ownership of you. In fact, you need to be incredibly conscious of taking ownership of everything that you are. And I do mean everything. Those few extra pounds, the nose you think is too big, your ginger hair or freckled skin. Whatever it is that you are insecure about, it's time that you showed up and took ownership. Because the moment you do your world will change.

But what does that look like? Why does it matter?

If someone parks a limo in the road outside your house, hands you the keys and tells you it is yours, what would you do? You're not just gonna put the keys in the ignition and leave it in the road. You are going to put that thing in a garage and get it insured. You will make sure that it is in a place where it is safe from weather and your jealous neighbour. Those are the things that you do when you take ownership of something. You make sure that they are protected because you value them. Then when you drive around town you don't look around as if you've stolen the thing. You drive with style and confidence. You are bold and comfortable because it belongs to you. *That* is what ownership looks like.

Now I know what you're thinking. That's easy to do with a limo, but I what I have is the equivalent of a car built before world war two. But the beautiful thing about ownership is that it does not depend on the object. It is not the thing being owned that you have to worry about, all you have to do is claim it. You've seen teenagers when they get their first car. Even if it is an old rust-bucket they drive around beaming with pride. Why? Because they know that what they have is theirs. It belongs to them and so they take ownership of it.

You have to do the same. You must take ownership of every part of you because in doing so you will keep it secure. You no longer have to be insecure about your weight if you know that that is where you are at right now. That doesn't mean you don't work for change though. It doesn't give you an excuse for stagnancy. You take accountability for your change and growth as much as you do for your present state. But in taking ownership you work towards polishing your pride, not getting rid of your low self-esteem. The difference may sound semantic, but the implications are enormous. The one allows you to work towards something and get somewhere good. The other makes it feel like you are just running away from something. And when you are running away then the only direction that matters is away – even if that means you run in circles.

Make a change today. Own yourself once more and be amazed at the rush that comes with it. With ownership comes confidence.

Chapter 23:

10 Habits of Unsuccessful People

Highly successful people (in any of the many ways that "success" can be defined) seem to recognize a few basic principles. The most important of these is that your energy, not your time, is restricted each day and must be carefully controlled.

Here are 10 of the most popular self-imposed blocks that have a troll on your success. If you come across one, use it as a cue to reevaluate, reflect, and change direction.

1. Worry of the Most Unlikely Outcome.

Despite its label as a "maladaptive trait," worrying has an evolutionary connection to intelligence. This is why, according to Jeremy Coplan, lead author of a study published of Frontiers in Evolutionary Neuroscience, effective people are naturally nervous.

Whatever the case may be, to work correctly, you must be able to distinguish between which fears are worth reacting to and which are your brain's attempt to "prepare" you for survival by conjuring up the most severe possible risk. This is an antiquated, animalistic mechanism that is useless in everyday life. Highly effective people should not spend their time worrying about the things that are least likely to happen.

2. Just Talking the Talk.

"I'm preparing to do this and that." What's better than announcing on social media that you're starting a business? Putting it into action.

Entrepreneur Derek Sivers argued in his 2010 TED talk, "Keep Your Goals to Yourself," that disclosing your intentions can be detrimental rather than inspiring. People will sometimes applaud you just for stating your purpose, he said, and this applause, ironically, may drain your motivation to carry out the plans you've just outlined.

"Psychotherapists have discovered that telling others your goal and having them embrace it is known as a 'social reality,'" Sivers explained in his talk. "The mind is deceived into believing it has already been accomplished. Then, after you've had your satisfaction, you're less likely to put in the necessary effort."

There's nothing wrong with expressing your happiness. However, try to keep your mouth shut before you have good news, not just good intentions.

3. Ruminating and Not Doing Anything About It.

Reflecting becomes ruminating as the intention to act dissolves in favor of constantly replaying certain situations or issues through your mind.

Self-awareness is common among highly successful individuals, or at least it should be. This means they devote a significant amount of time to reflecting on their behavior and experiences and determining how they can change. However, they do not waste mental energy pondering what went wrong rather than consciously modifying what needs to be changed to fix the issue.

4. Choosing the Wrong People To Spend Time With.

The people you hang out with can either inspire you to be your best self or bring out your worst traits. Spend time with people who can motivate you to make the changes you want to make in your life. Do you want to fail at that goal completely? If it's the case, spend time with people who gloat about their bad habits. People get their energy from each other. Always remember that you are the average of the 5 people that you spend most of your time with.

5. Being Resentful for Taking Time for Themselves.

People who have experienced any degree of success understand that it is a multi-faceted operation. You won't be able to work at your best if you're tired, undernourished, or experiencing some other sort of extreme imbalance in your life.

As a result, highly successful individuals are just as dedicated to relaxation and health as work and efficiency. They don't stress themselves up about how much they should have done in a three-day weekend or why they shouldn't take time off when they need it.

6. Constantly Concentrating on the Negative.

It's mind-boggling to focus on the negative aspects of life because it'll only make you feel worse. You don't have to believe that life is simple to concentrate on the positive. You should maintain a rational viewpoint without always pointing out the flaws in everything you see.

We've all met someone who is still complaining about something. "Ugh, it rained this morning, and my shoes were soaked through and through." Yes, that's a disappointment. You won't be able to affect the weather, unfortunately. You should put on a new pair of shoes if you want to.

It's fine if you're having a rough day; we're all irritable at times; everybody gets irritable now and then. However, you are living a poor life if you despise anything. That's what there is to it.

7. Justifying Their Place in Life.

Taking on exceptional work also elicits questions and, at times, judgments from those who don't believe in your project or are suspicious of its long-term viability. Constantly feeling the need to explain or justify your role in life, on the other hand, is not only exhausting but also unnecessary. Highly effective people understand that you can't get approval from people who don't want it.

8. Allowing Themselves To Be Sucked Into a State of Laziness.

We've all had times when we've been compelled to cancel plans. Leaving the house, even for something "fun," can feel like a Herculean task at times.

However, it is fresh and novel experiences that make life so beautiful. You aren't fully involved in your own life when you succumb to laziness, which is unfair to your friends, family, spouse, and those who want to share it with you.

9. Worrying That Isn't Essential and Unregulated Thought Patterns.

Worrying is among the most common ways people drain their energy doing. It is the act of anticipating the worst-case scenario and assuming that it is not only probable but most likely.

Worrying does not make you more equipped to deal with life's challenges instead, it makes you more likely to build your fears. You'd be surprised to learn that 99.9% of your worries were baseless and never "came true" if you made a list of everything you've ever worried about in your life.

If you just made a list of everything you didn't care about in life, you'd find that worrying didn't change anything; it just sapped your energy at the moment. The only thing it has done for you is that it made things more complicated, twisted, and less fun. It is not only ineffective, but completely pointless as well. Highly successful people learn to concentrate on something else rather than spend their time worrying about what could go wrong.

10. There Is Just Too Much Optimistic Thought.

It's self-evident that no one achieves remarkable success without first confronting destructive thought patterns. What's less evident is that highly successful people don't partake in excessive positive thinking, which can be arbitrary, distorted, and even distracting in excess. Worse, they set themselves up for failure or disappointment by thinking too positively. Instead, highly successful people understand the power of neutral thought, which means they don't try to make life into something.

Conclusion

If you don't want to be an unsuccessful person, you need to make a conscious effort to avoid doing these things. Focus on the habits that would bring you positive change instead, which we will discuss in another segment.

Chapter 24:

5 Ways Quitting Something Can Bring You Joy

Do you ever wonder if you will ever be truly happy in your life? Do you wonder if happiness is just a hoax and success is an illusion? Do you feel like they don't exist? I know a friend who felt like this a little while ago. At the time, she was making a six-figure income, was working for her dream company (Apple), and had a flexible work schedule. Despite all this, she was miserable. She would have never been able to quit my job if not for the practice she got from quitting little things.

Of all the things that she tried, quitting these seven little things made her the happiest.

1. Quit Reading the News

News headlines are usually about happenings around the world. Most times, they are negative. Negative headlines make for better stories than positive headlines. Would you read a headline that says 'Electric Chair Makes a Comeback' or a headline that says 'Legislation debate in Tennessee'? See what I mean.

Journalists have to write stories that interest us. I can't blame them for that. Changing the time that I caught up on the news helped me be more positive during the day. Start reading inspirational posts first thing in the morning instead of news. You can still catch the news later, around 11 am instead of at 6 am.

2. Quit Hunching Your Shoulders

This boosted my confidence levels.

We hunch our shoulders and take up as little space as possible when we feel nervous and not too comfortable. This is body language 101.

Keeping a posture, opening up your shoulders will make you feel more confident during the day. But, I must admit it will make you more tired than usual. It will take you at least a total of 45 days before you start doing this effortlessly.

3. Quit Keeping a Corporate Face at Work

We are all trained not to show real feelings at work. Having a corporate face is good for corporate, not for you. Smiling all day, even when you are upset, will lift your mood. It will make you feel better sooner. Studies have shown that smiling makes you happy.

4. Quit Writing Huge Goals

It is better to write and work towards achievable goals before starting to write our stretch goals. Stretch goals are great to push ourselves. But, we all need achievable goals to boost confidence and to have successes that we can build momentum on. This can be hard for you if you are an overachiever.

5. Quit Eating Fries and Eat Oranges Instead

Fries are comfort food for a lot of people. But eating them saps energy.

Eat oranges instead of fries every time you feel down and feel the need for comfort food. This not only boosts your energy but will also help you lose some pounds if you want to. Plus, this will give you energy and clarity of mind.

Chapter 25:

How Luck Is Created From Success

Success and luck, just two simple words with meaning more profound than the ocean. These words are interrelated. For everyone, success has a different meaning because everyone has a distant dream to fulfill. Some people want a simple life, but some want to live with the luxuries of life. "Dream big" we all have heard this; setting high goals for the future proves that you believe in yourself, that you can do it after it is only you that can make you a success. Some people believe in luck, but luck goes hand in hand with hard work, determination, creativity. To earn the victory, you will always have to work hard, and you can't just leave everything on luck. But how can you make your luck from success? One may ask.

There are a few simple steps to make your luck. When you face a failure, don't just give up yet, don't ever assume that you can't do anything about the situation. It would be best if you decided to take control. It would help if you believed that you could handle the situation and fix the problems; when has giving up ever been suitable for someone's life. When you decide to take control of things, things turn out to be just fine.

As I said before, believing in yourself is a significant part of making your luck. Do something now. Stop postponing things you want to do, gather some willpower, and do it now before it's too late. Another thing you can do to learn to be lucky is to sit back and make a list of various options; if you can't follow up on one of the options, then go for the other one. Think about as many options as you can; just be creative.

When something holds us back, it is tough for us to move forward, or when you are stuck at the same routine and are not doing anything to move forward, luck can do nothing about your laziness. Take out time for yourself and decide about how you will move forward, how you will grow. Consider every single alternative out there. After determining what you want to do in the future, seek the opportunities. Whenever you think you have a chance, take action; now is not the time to sit back and watch; it is the time to run and grab that opportunity because you never know when the next time will come.

Successful people are committed to the fact that they want to be in control of their lives; that is how you make your luck from your success. It's all about believing in yourself.

Chapter 26:

6 Ways To Attract Anything You Want In Life

It is common human nature that one wants whatever one desires in life. People work their ways to get what they need or want. This manifestation of wanting to attract things is almost in every person around us. A human should be determined to work towards his goal or dreams through sheer hard work and will. You have to work towards it step by step because no matter what we try or do, we will always have to work for it in the end. So, it is imperative to work towards your goal and accept the fact that you can't achieve it without patience and dedication.

We have to start by improving ourselves day by day. A slight change a day can help us make a more considerable change for the future. We should feel the need to make ourselves better in every aspect. If we stay the way we are, tomorrow, we will be scared of even a minor change. We feel scared to let go of our comfort zone and laziness. That way, either we or our body can adapt to the changes that make you better, that makes you attract better.

1. **Start With Yourself First**

We all know that every person is responsible for his own life. That is why people try to make everything revolves around them. It's no secret that everyone wants to associate with successful, healthy, and charming people. But, what about ourselves? We should also work on ourselves to become the person others would admire. That is the type of person people love. He can also easily attract positive things to himself. It becomes easier to be content with your desires. We need to get ourselves together and let go of all the things we wouldn't like others doing.

2. Have A Clear Idea of Your Wants

Keeping in mind our goal is an easy way to attract it. Keep reminding yourself of all the pending achievements and all the dreams. It helps you work towards it, and it enables you to attract whatever you want. Make sure that you are aware of your intentions and make them count in your lives. You should always make sure to have a crystal-clear idea of your mindset, so you will automatically work towards it. It's the most basic principle to start attracting things to you.

3. Satisfaction With Your Achievements

It is hard to stop wanting what you once desired with your heart, but you should always be satisfied with anything you are getting. This way, when you attract more, you become happier. So, it is one of the steps to draw things, be thankful. Be thankful for what you are getting and what you haven't. Every action has a reason for itself. It doesn't mean just to let it be. Work for your goals but also acknowledge the ones already achieved by you in life. That way you will always be happy and satisfied.

4. Remove Limitations and Obstacles

We often limit ourselves during work. We have to know that there is no limit to working for what you want when it comes to working for what you want. You remove the obstacles that are climbing their way to your path. It doesn't mean to overdo yourselves, but only to check your capability. That is how much pressure you can handle and how far you can go in one go. If you put your boundaries overwork, you will always do the same amount, thus, never improving further. Push yourself a little more each time you work for the things you want in life.

5. Make Your Actions Count

We all know that visualizing whatever you want makes it easier to get. But we still cannot ignore the fact that it will not reach us unless we do some hard work and action. Our actions speak louder than words, and they speak louder than our thoughts. So, we have to make sure that our actions are built of our brain image. That is the way you could attract the things you want in life. Action is an essential rule for attracting anything you want in life.

6. Be Optimistic About Yourselves

Positivity is an essential factor when it comes to working towards your goals or dreams. When you learn to be optimistic about almost everything, you will notice that everything will make you satisfied. You will attract positive things and people. Negative vibes will leave you disappointed in yourself and everyone around you. So, you will have to practice positivity. It may not be easy at first while everyone around you is pushing you to negativity. That is where your test begins, and you have to prove yourself to them and yourself. And before you know it, you are attracting things you want.

Conclusion

Everyone around us wants to attract what they desire, but you have to start with yourself first. You only have to focus on yourself to achieve what you want. And attracting things will come naturally to you. Make sure you work for your dreams and goals with all your dedication and determination. With these few elements, you will be attracting anything you want.

Chapter 27:

How to Share Your Talent

Hi everybody! I hope everyone is doing well. Today, we're going to talk about sharing your talent to the world. As humans, it is so natural to us to feel that we want to share a part of ourselves to the world around us through one way or another. We have this yearning to create or produce something that will benefit other people. We feel a sense of fulfillment in knowing that we did something to positively impact other people's lives. And one way to do this is by sharing our talents.

So, let's get to the steps on how you'll be able to share your talents.

First, you have to discover your talent. Know what you can offer. Believe that you have something in you that you can offer to the world to be the light that it needs and find it. Listen to your intuition and subconscious mind. Most of the time, your intuition knows what you have and how you'll be able to let it out. Know that everyone is unique and the world needs your authenticity and whatever that you can give. Don't allow society or cultural norms to dictate what you should be doing or where you should be good at.

Next, practice what you believe you're good at. Discovering your talents doesn't always mean that you'll be instantly great at it. You still need to make efforts to hone them. Take your time to practice and focus on your progress. Even the most talented musicians or athletes that ever walk this on planet spent so much time practicing and improving their crafts. So, don't give up if you feel like you are not going anywhere with your talent.

Third step is to be open to all possibilities. Sometimes, we want to be really good at one thing and we end up not giving ourselves a chance to be open to other opportunities. Life is full of surprises. Don't limit yourself in one field because you won't know what are the other things you're good at if you'll be so afraid to try something new. You're probably pursuing to hone your talent in music but you might also be good in writing. You won't know that you write really well if you don't give yourself a chance to try it. So, be open to all the possibilities and don't ever hold back.

Next step is to find your tribe. Your tribe is the people that share the same visions as you. They are the ones that believe in you and support you in your endeavors as you hone your talents. They make you feel that you and your talents are valued. And you do all these to them too. You support one another. Being with the right people that empower you to realize your full potential is an important part of your journey. So, if you'll ever find your tribe, stay with them and you'll surely go places.

Fifth step is to get yourself out in the world. Don't hesitate to show yourself and what you can offer. Remember that there's only one you in the whole world and that is your power. Even if some people will reject you and your work, there will always be people that you will inspire by just merely showing up. Don't let every rejection stop you in sharing your talent. Many successful authors have faced multiple rejections before their works got published. A lot of great actors and actresses have experienced failed auditions before they get to perform in televisions and cinemas. Many engineers have received bad grades when they were students before they got their degree. But they all made it to where they are now because they did not let any of the rejections they received to stop them in honing their talents and pursuing their dreams. So, don't give up on your talents. With perseverance and hardwork, you will also shine and light someone's world.

When you share your talent, you're not only making a positive impact on other people's lives but it also improves your own being. There is no other more fulfilling feeling in the world than to know that you've made someone's day a little brighter by sharing a part of yourself. As humans, we only have one chance to walk on this planet. And if we could make this world a little better than how we find it, that one chance is totally worth it. Life is beautiful as they say. But it will be even better if we share it with others.

Chapter 28:
What To Do When You Feel Like Your Work is not Good Enough

Feeling like your work is not good enough is very common; your nerves can get better of you at any time throughout your professional life. There is nothing wrong with nerves; It tells you that you care about improving and doing well. Unfortunately, too much nervousness can lead to major self-doubt, and that can be crippling. You are probably very good at your work, and when even once you take a dip, you think that things are not like how they seem to you. If this is something you're feeling, then you're not alone, and this thing is known as Imposter Syndrome. This term is used to describe self-doubt and inadequacy. This one thing leaves people fearing that there might be someone who will expose them. The more pressure you apply to yourself, the more dislocation is likely to occur. You create more anxiety, which creates more fear, which creates more self-doubt. You don't have to continue like this. You can counter it.

Beyond Work

If your imposter syndrome affects you at work, you should take some time out and start focusing on other areas of your life. There are chances that there is something in your personal life that is hindering your work life. This could be anything your sleep routine, friends, diet, or even your relationships. There is a host of external factors that can affect your performance. If there are some boxes you aren't ticking, then there is a high chance of you not performing well at work.

You're Better Than You Think

When you're being crippled by self-doubt, the first thing you have to think about is why you were hired in the first place. The interviewers saw something in you that they believed would improve the business.

So, do you think they would recruit someone who can't do the job? No, they saw your talent, they saw something in you, and you will come good.

When you find yourself in this position, take a moment to write down a few things that you believe led to you being in the role you are now. What did those recruiters see? What did your boss recognize in you? You can also look back on a period of time where you were clicking and felt victorious. What was different then versus now? Was there an external issue like diet, exercise, socializing, etc.?

Check Yourself Before You Wreck Yourself

A checklist might be of some use to you. If you have a list to measure yourself against, then it gives you more than just one thing to judge yourself against. We're far too quick to doubt ourselves and criticize harshly.

The most obvious checklist in terms of work is technical or hard skills, but soft skills matter, too. It's also important to remember that while you're technically proficient now, things move quickly, and you'll reach a point where everything changes, and you have to keep up. You might not ever excel at something, but you can accept the change and adapt to the best of your ability.

It matters that you're hard-working, loyal, honest, and trustworthy. There's more to judge yourself on than just your job. Even if you make a mistake, it's temporary, and you can fix it.

Do you take criticism well? Are you teachable? Easy to coach? Soft skills count for something, which you can look to even at your lowest point and recognize you have strengths.

When you're struggling through a day, week, or even a month, take one large step backward and think about what it is you're unhappy with. What's causing your unhappiness, and how can you improve it?

It comes down to how well you know yourself. If you're clear on what your values are and what you want out of life, then you're going to be fine. If the organization you work for can't respect your values and harness your strengths, then you're better off elsewhere. So, it is extremely important to take time out for that self check-in there could be times you talk to yourself in negative light. Checking in with yourself regularly and not feeding yourself negativity could be one-step forward.

Chapter 29:

Stop Dwelling on Things

It's 5 p.m., the deadline for an important work project is at 6, and all you can think about is the fight you had with the next-door neighbor this morning. You're dwelling. "It's natural to look inward," but while most people pull out when they've done it enough, an overthinker will stay in the loop."

Ruminating regularly often leads to depression. So, if you're prone to obsessing (and you know who you are), try these tactics to head off the next full-tilt mental spin cycle...

1.Distract Yourself

Go and exercise, scrub the bathtub spotless, put on music and dance, do whatever engrosses you, and do it for at least 10 minutes. That's the minimum time required to break a cycle of thoughts.

2.Make a Date to Dwell

Tell yourself you can obsess all you want from 6 to 7 p.m., but until then, you're banned. "By 6 p.m., you'll probably be able to think things through more clearly,"

3. 3 Minutes of Mindfulness

For one minute, eyes closed, acknowledge all the thoughts going through your mind. For the next minute, just focus on your breathing. Spend the last minute expanding your awareness from your breath to your entire body. "Paying attention in this way gives you the room to see the questions you're asking yourself with less urgency and to reconsider them from a different perspective,"

4.The Best and Worst Scenarios

Ask yourself...

"What's the worst that could happen?" and "How would I cope?" Visualizing yourself handling the most extreme outcome should alleviate some anxiety. Then consider the likelihood that the worst will occur.

Next, imagine the best possible outcome; by this point, you'll be in a more positive frame of mind and better able to assess the situation more realistically.

5. Call a Friend

Ask a friend or relative to be your point person when your thoughts start to speed out of control.

6. Is it worth it?

If you find that your mind is fixated on a certain situation, ask yourself if the dwelling is worth your time.

'Ask yourself if looking over a certain situation will help you accept it, learn from it and find closure,' 'If the answer is no, you should make a conscious effort to shelve the issue and move on from it.'

7. Identify your anxiety trigger

There may be a pattern in your worries, and this means you can help identify potential causes and use practice preventative measures.

'For many of us, rumination will occur after a trigger, so it is important to identify what it is,' 'For example, if you have to give a presentation at work and the last one you didn't go to plan, this can cause rumination and anxiety.'

Chapter 30:

10 Habits of Adele

There's no denying it, Adele Laurie Blue Adkins, better known as Adele is a musical legend. She is an English singer-songwriter and all-time great vocalist with excellent lyrical and passionate composing skills. Adele is one of the world's best-selling music artist, having sold over 120 million records worldwide.

With her exceptional voice and songwriting skills, the singer from a rough side of the town has captivated the hearts of millions of people. Adele got her admiration as an award-winning music legend, but moreover, there is much more from a lady who has overcome adversity to reach the top.

Here are 10 habits of Adele that will serve your learning journey.

1. It's Far From Easy

Criticism came thick and quick after Adele signed her first record deal because of her physical appearance. Many people, including Record label executives and high-profile designers publicly chastised her as "too fat" while suggesting weight loss to attract a larger fan base. Adele didn't let such criticism weigh in her talent as she unapologetically made hits after hits. Just like Adele, don't try to be anything or anyone but yourself.

2. Commitment Is Success

Despite constant pressure from the media to conform to their ludicrous notions of what women in the spotlight should look like, Adele chose her path and remained committed to being herself. This honesty is one of the attributes that Adele's fans admire. Such personality traits will breed your success.

3. It's Okay To Be Sad After a Breakup

When a relationship ends, you believe in acting tough and putting on a solid face. You're convinced on being tough to appear as you're suffering less than your ex-partners to win in some way. Adele defies expectations by telling her exes and the rest of the world about her grief without fear. She exemplifies humanity and vulnerability through her music.

4. Don't Take Life Too Seriously

It's okay to laugh at yourself or a hilarious scenario from time to time. Whether she's being teased in an interview or asked whether she wants to be a Bond Girl, Adele always respond with "Hahaha". She is quick to laugh, and her laugh is contagious.

5. Adversity Doesn't Stop Anything

Allow your pain to drive your mission. What if Adele waited till everything was back to normal before recording? All in all, people rushed to get her music, which she recorded in her misery. Every minute, every day, life happens and so should you commit to completing your projects without unconditionally.

6. Mirror Your Brand To Reflect Longevity

Say it quietly: Adele's tracks would have hit ten, twenty, or even fifty years ago. To call them timeless is a bit of a stretch. The fact may be that they're essentially personal because we believe that her music is basically from her life or personal experiences. However, Adele is always true to herself and then she sings authentically which is a formidable brand blend.

7. There Are Other Better Places Than the Spotlight

Adele doesn't constantly boost her social media presence and create "news" for constant consumption. Instead, she vanishes to do bizarre things like live and breathe and then reappears when she has something she hopes people would appreciate. It's tempting to feel the need to keep fulfilling it, but according to Adele, being true to yourself is more fulfilling.

8. Build Your Team, Not Just Yourself

When a technical issue nearly derailed her performance at Grammy Awards, Adele didn't cast an evil eye at her sound engineer. Not only did she make herself appear good by ending her performance properly, she also made her entire team look excellent. The question is, what do you do when life tosses you a curveball that you can't control?

9. Keep Going

Even when things are out of your control, it's easy to quit when everything seems to go wrong. But your perseverance will be rewarded!

10. Remember Where You Came From

Don't let your past or upbringing hold you back from achieving your goals in the future. Success is defined not by what you have as a child but by your level of commitment and work ethic over time. However, once you get there, don't forget where you come from.

Conclusion

You are characterized not by your physical appearance but by how you treat people and the words you use while communicating with everyone. Hence, just like Adele, have the confidence to pursue your aspirations. You never know where the road may take you.

Chapter 31:

Discomfort Is Temporary

It's easy to get hopeless when things get a little overwhelming. It's easy to give up because you feel you don't have the strength or resources to continue. But where you stop is actually the start you have been looking for since the beginning.

Do you know what you should do when you are broken? You should relish it. You should use it. Because if you know you are broken, congratulations, you have found your limitations.

Now as you know what stopped you last time, you can work towards mending it. You can start to reinforce the breach and you should be able to fill in the cracks in no time.

Life never repeats everything. One day you feel the lowest and the next might bring you the most unpredictable gifts.

The world isn't all sunshine and rainbows. It is a very mean and nasty place to be in. But what can you do now when you are in it? Nothing? Never!

You have to endure the pain, the stress, the discomfort till you are comfortable with the discomfort. It doesn't make any sense, right? But listen to me.

You have a duty towards yourself. You have a duty towards your loved ones. You are expected to rise above all odds and be something no one has ever been before you. I know it might be a little too much to ask for, but, you have to understand your purpose.

Your purpose isn't just to sit on your back and the opportunities and blessings keep coming, knocking at your door, just so you can give up one more time and turn them down.

Things are too easy to reject and neglect but always get hard when you finally step up and go for them. But remember, every breathtaking view is from the top of a hill, but the trek to the top is always tiring. But when you get to the top, you find every cramp worth it.

If you are willing to put yourself through anything, discomfort and temporary small intervals of pain won't affect you in any way. As long as you believe that the experience will bring you to a new level.

If you are interested in the unknown, then you have to break barriers and cross your limits. Because every path that leads to success is full of them. But then and only then you will find yourself in a place where you are unbreakable.

You need to realize that your life is better than most people out there. You need to embrace the pain because all this is temporary. But when you are finally ready to embrace the pain, you are already on your way to a superior being.

Life is all about taking stands because we all get all kinds of blows. But we always need to dig in and keep fighting till we have found the gems or have found our last breath.

The pain and discomfort will subside one day, but if you quit, then you are already on the end of your rope.

Chapter 32:

How To Rid Yourself of Distraction

Distraction and disaster sound rather similar.

It is a worldwide disorder that you are probably suffering from.

Distraction is robbing you of precious time during the day.

Distraction is robbing you of time that you should be working on your goals.

If you don't rid yourself of distraction, you are in big trouble.

It is a phenomenon that most employees are only productive 3 out of 8 hours at the office.

If you could half your distractions, you could double your productivity.

How far are you willing to go to combat distraction?

How badly do you want to achieve proper time management?

If you know you only have an hour a day to work, would it help keep you focused?

Always focus on your initial reason for doing work in the first place.

After all that reason is still there until you reach your goal.

Create a schedule for your day to keep you from getting distracted.

Distractions are everywhere.

It pops up on your phone.

It pops up from people wanting to chat at work.

It pops up in the form of personal problems.

Whatever it may be, distractions are abound.

The only cure is clear concentration.

To have clear concentration it must be something you are excited about.

To have clear knowledge that this action will lead you to something exciting.

If you find the work boring, It will be difficult for you to concentrate too long.

Sometimes it takes reassessing your life and admitting your work is boring for you to consider a change in direction.

Your goal will have more than one path.

Some paths boring, some paths dangerous, some paths redundant, and some paths magical.

You may not know better until you try.

After all the journey is everything.

If reaching your goal takes decades of work that makes you miserable, is it really worth it?

The changes to your personality may be irreversible.

Always keep the goal in mind whilst searching for an enjoyable path to attain it.

After all if you are easily distracted from your goal, then do you really want it?

Ask yourself the hard questions.
Is this something you really want? Or is this something society wants for you?

Many people who appear successful to society are secretly miserable.
Make sure you are aware of every little detail of your life.
Sit down and really decide what will make you happy at the end of your life.

What work will you be really happy to do?
What are the causes and people you would be happy to serve?
How much money you want?
What kind of relationships you want?
If you can build a clear vision of this life for you, distractions will become irrelevant.
Irrelevant because nothing will be able to distract you from your perfect vision.

Is what you are doing right now moving you towards that life?
If not stop, and start doing the things what will.
It really is that simple.

Anyone who is distracted for too long from the task in hand has no business doing that task. They should instead be doing something that makes them happy.

We can't be happy all the time otherwise we wouldn't be able to recognize it.

But distraction is a clear indicator you may not be on the right path for you.

Clearly define your path and distraction will be powerless.

Chapter 33:

Blaming Others In Your Life For Your Mistakes

When something goes wrong, are you more likely to own up to the mistakes you made, or play the blame game?

Many people are quick to point fingers and play the blame game. In fact, recent research has shown that we *expect* this behavior to happen. We expect to experience others engaging in blame-shifting, placing the blame on others for their own mistakes.

My hands aren't clean. I've blamed people for my own mistakes more than once, that's for sure. Why? It's easy.

Simply put, it's much easier to place the blame on someone else than to take full responsibility for your actions. It's also easier to blame someone for our actions rather than take a deeper look at why we made the mistake that we did and face possible consequences — whether it was something you did at work or something that happened during a tiff between you and your partner. Blame shifting takes less effort, and it's easier on us emotionally — at least in the moment.

"Blame is like another defense mechanism,". "We could call it denial or projection, because it helps us preserve our sense of self-esteem or pride by avoiding awareness of our own issues."

Why do we use defense mechanisms? To protect ourselves — whether it's from criticism, negative consequences, attention, whatever it is you're afraid of. You might even be in denial that you are, in fact, the one who's making mistakes.

"We can think of it as a tool we use when we're in attack mode,".
Alternatively, she notes that some people blame others in an attempt to hurt them — which is certainly not cool!

Furthermore, it's possible that you might have some deep rooted negative experiences from your childhood that make you predisposed to acting in this way. "Psychologically, we can also see that attachment issues can create problems that manifest when we grow up,". "Insecure and ambivalent attachments can lead to us not accepting responsibilities and finding blaming easier."

Seldom does blaming others for our mistakes come without consequences. It might feel like we're winning in the moment, benefitting ourselves when we don't take responsibility for our actions, but that's definitely not the case in the long run. Blaming others can, and likely will, backfire on you, leaving you wishing you never played the blame game in the first place.

If it wasn't obvious, those you blame *will* realize it, and they're not going to be happy that you're not owning up to your own blunders. As with many toxic behaviors, acknowledging that you have the problem is the first step to addressing it. Even acknowledging it might not be easy for you, since finally, you'll have to take the blame yourself, and hold yourself accountable for your actions. If you're a chronic blamer, it might have been a while since you took responsibility for yourself.

We have to learn to be able to hold ourselves accountable for mistakes big and small, even though it can be scary. It's not easy to own up to our errors, but without a doubt, it's the right thing to do.

Chapter 34:

Becoming High Achievers

By becoming high achievers we become high off life, what better feeling is there than aiming for something you thought was unrealistic and then actually hitting that goal.

What better feeling is there than declaring we will do something against the perceived odds and then actually doing it.

To be a high achiever you must be a believer,

You must believe in yourself and believe that dream is possible for you.

It doesn't matter what anyone else thinks , as long as you believe,

To be a high achiever we must hunger to achieve.

To be an action taker.

Moving forward no matter what.

High achievers do not quit.

Keeping that vision in their minds eye until it becomes reality, no matter what.

Your biggest dream is protected by fear , loss and pain.

We must conquer all 3 of these impostors to walk through the door.

Not many do , most are still fighting fear and if they lose the battle, they quit.

Loss and pain are part of life.

Losses are hard on all of us.

Whether we lose possessions, whether we lose friends, whether we lose our jobs, or whether we lose family members.

Losing doesn't mean you have lost.

Losses are may be a tough pill to swallow, but they are essential because we cannot truly succeed until we fail.

We can't have the perfect relationship if we stay in a toxic one, and we can't have the life we desire until we make room by letting go of the old.

The 3 imposters that cause us so much terror are actually the first signs of our success.

So walk through fear in courage , look at loss as an eventual gain, and know that the pain is part of the game and without it you would be weak.

Becoming a high achiever requires a single minded focus on your goal, full commitment and an unnatural amount of persistence and work.

We must define what high achievement means to us individually, set the bar high and accept nothing less.

The achievement should not be money as money is not our currency but a tool.

The real currency is time and your result is the time you get to experience the world's places and products , so the result should always be that.

The holiday home , the fast car and the lifestyle of being healthy and wealthy, those are merely motivations to work towards. Like Carrots on a stick.

High achievement is individual to all of us, it means different things to each of us,

But if we are going to go for it we might as well go all out for the life we want, should we not?

I don't think we beat the odds of 1 in 400 trillion to be born, just to settle for mediocrity, did we?

Being a high achiever is in your DNA , if you can beat the odds , you can beat anything.

It is all about self-belief and confidence, we must have the confidence to take the action required and often the risk.

Risk is difficult for people and it's a difficult tight rope to walk. The line between risk and recklessness is razor thin.

Taking risks feels unnatural, not surprisingly as we all grew up in a health and safety bubble with all advice pointing towards safe and secure ways.

But the reward is often in the risk and sometimes a leap of blind faith is required. This is what stops most of us - the fear of the unknown.

The truth is the path to success is foggy and we can only ever see one step ahead , we have to imagine the result and know it's somewhere down this foggy path and keep moving forward with our new life in mind.

Know that we can make it but be aware that along the path we will be met by fear , loss and pain and the bigger our goal the bigger these monsters will be.

The top achievers financially are fanatical about their work and often work 100+ hours per week.

Some often work day and night until a project is successful.

Being a high achiever requires giving more than what is expected, standing out for the high standard of your work because being known as number 1 in your field will pay you abundantly.

Being an innovator, thinking outside the box for better practices, creating superior products to your competition because quality is more rewarding than quantity.

Maximizing the quality of your products and services to give assurance to your customers that your company is the number 1 choice.

What can we do differently to bring a better result to the table and a better experience for our customers?

We must think about questions like that because change is inevitable and without thinking like that we get left behind, but if we keep asking that, we can successfully ride the wave of change straight to the beach of our desired results.

The route to your success is by making people happy because none of us can do anything alone, we must earn the money and to earn it we must make either our employers or employees and customers happy.

To engage in self-promotion and positive interaction with those around us, we must be polite and positive with everyone, even with our competition.

Because really the only competition is ourselves and that is all we should focus on.

Self-mastery, how can I do better than yesterday?

What can I do different today that will improve my circumstances for tomorrow.

Little changes add up to a big one.

The belief and persistence towards your desired results should be 100%, I will carry on until… is the right attitude.

We must declare to ourselves that we will do this , we don't yet know how but we know that we will.

Because high achievers like yourselves know that to make it you must endure and persist untill you win.

High achievers have an unnatural grit and thick skin , often doing what others won't, putting in the extra hours when others don't.

After you endure loss and conquer pain , the sky is the limit, and high achievers never settle until they are finished.

CPSIA information can be obtained
at www.ICGtesting.com
Printed in the USA
LVHW080637290122
709444LV00016B/1508